When Virtue Meets A Shattered Dream

ISBN: 978-978-789-084-4

PUBLISHED IN NIGERIA BY:

Ultimate Index Book Publishers Ltd.

Nigeria

DESIGN AND PRINTED BY:

Favtex International Resources
Tel: +2348064915824, +2349077035033
Email: favtexintl@gmail.com

Peace Global Revival Networks (PGRN)

Table of Contents

Preface 4

Foreword 5

DEDICATION 8

ACKNOWLEDGMENTS 9

CHAPTER ONE 10

INTRODUCTION 10

CHAPTER TWO 18

THE BIG QUESTION 18

CHAPTER THREE 22

LOVE WILL WAKEN THE DEAD 22

CHAPTER FOUR 28

FAITH CONQUERS EVEN THROUGH THE WATERS DEEP 28

CHAPTER FIVE 36

SELF CONTROL MAKES PALACE THROUGH PRISON ... 36

CHAPTER SIX 40

ENDURANCE WILL REACH THE FINISH LINE 40

CHAPTER SEVEN 44

JOY PREVAILS THROUGH THE PAIN 44

CHAPTER EIGHT 48

PEACE WILL STILL RAGING STORMS 48

CHAPTER NINE 52

GOODNESS SPARKLES THROUGH THE NEED 52

CHAPTER TEN 54

MEEKNESS AND GENTLENESS: THE KEYS THAT CONNECT FACE TO FACE WITH GOD! 54
CHAPTER ELEVEN 58
THE FEAR OF THE LORD WILL GUARD YOU! 58
TO YOU MY READER 62
References 64
ABOUT THE AUTHOR 66

Preface

I sincerely believe that the worst thing that can happen to any writer, is writing when he has not been called or anointed to do so. Frankly speaking, it was never in my plans whatsoever to put down a piece of work like this.

The book, "When Virtue Meets A Shattered Dream", was a divine instruction which I decided to respond to. I said to myself, "if this is the will of God, then I can't run away from it", while I trusted Him to help me shoulder the responsibilities involved in having it written.

It is a book that talks about How God's Virtue can transform you, and make you the wonderful person He created you to be. And, as well as, how you can become life possessor of it. It is a product of many years of prayers and commitment to God.

I did my best to use clear, simple, and understandable words, as possible. It speaks from the heart of scriptures, and have scriptural references, for your spiritual growth. There is also a powerful addendum at the end of each chapter, for your nourishment!

Foreword

The virtue of God will pour down just like the rain when the heavens are opened! Scripture says, "These are the generations of the heavens and of the earth when they were created, in the day that the Lord God made the earth and the heavens, and every plants of the field before it grew: for the Lord God hath not caused it to rain upon the earth, and there was not a man to till the ground." (Gen. 2:4-6). But things must be in place before God sends down the rain.

At the beginning of creation, God had not caused it to rain upon the earth. This does not mean that the earth was without water. For up till this time, God had caused a mist to come up from the earth to give moisture to the earth. However, there had been no down pour from the heavenlies. Why? Scripture says, "because there was not a man to till the ground". (Gen. 2:5)

There are certain things God has plans to do, has made provision for doing, and desires to do, but will not do, until man is in a place to receive what God intends to give.

Therefore, the virtue for man's blessings remains in the heavenlies, for God's safe keeping, while the need still stares at him – insistently, resistantly, and persistently. For the virtue won't be applied to the need until man's heart is in a position for God to act, according to His own laws of redemption, healing and deliverance.

There are blessings that God has in the heavenlies that may not be released to you, until you are in the proper position spiritually and relationally, to receive it.

Oh, you may have being experiencing a "mist", but in your spirit you have a restlessness that there must be something more! You have an inner knowing that you aren't fully where you ought to be. You have an uneasiness, a frustration that causes you to say, "why am I no further than this in my life?"

What is missing in your life is Virtue (the God kind of virtue). Rather than blaming your parents, your friends and associates, your boss, your country, or even your race, you are wise to ask yourself, "is God waiting on me to be in a different spiritual position before He pours out a blessing on my life?"

When you are in alignment with God and His purposes, He will open up the heavenlies and cause its virtue to rain on you. You will experience such an outpouring of God's blessings that you won't know how to contain them.

Therefore, Evangelist O'brian Wisdom, in this book titled, "When Virtue Meets A Shattered Dream," picks up his pen to provide a systematic, scripture-based, and ground-breaking approach on how to have an encounter with the Virtue that will transform your life. He is a person of holy integrity, anointed of God, and grounded in the word. Read this book prayerfully along with the scriptural references, and your life will turn around for good!

It is my prayer that through this book, great revival will be brought to the place where you are, and in your whole life – spirit, soul, and body!

Dr. Otogboro Samuel Reginald,
Pastor LDS – Church

DEDICATION

I dedicate this book to the Holy Triune, the source of my inspiration; the one who has placed a seal upon my life, for the ministry. He has held me up in difficult moments, and has always been my standby.

ACKNOWLEDGMENTS

First, I acknowledge my spiritual mentors Late Reinhard Bonke and Late Wesley L. Duewel (blessed memories) whose holy writs and lives helped shaped my Christian experience. I also acknowledge my parents, siblings, and friends for their immense support and contributions.

The typist, Miss Effiong Favour, is also acknowledged here, for painstakingly going through the manuscripts to correct all possible errors.

Finally, I acknowledge the editor, Pastor (Dr.) Otogboro Samuel Reginald for his good and quality finishing. He is simply superb!

WHEN VIRTUE MEETS

A SHATTERED DREAM

Evangelist Wisdom's Quotes

"What matters is not who you want to be, but who God wants to help you become!"

CHAPTER ONE

INTRODUCTION

In a school of arts, when a learner weaves a thread, and all of a sudden makes a mistake, the Master weaver takes the job from him. In his professionalness, he makes something even more beautiful out of the woven defects, that you know it that there has been a master's touch. This is exactly who God wills to be to us, as we journey through life. He wills to make us living holy artifacts in His mighty hands. And make out of us virtues of best refine. He also wills we visualize far beyond the horizon, to help us break through the limits that keep men in low spiritual estate.

In fact, our lives and dreams, are never already too good or too bad, too beautiful or not, to attract the Master's touch. And so, when an error has occurred somewhere in our lives, and we seem to be at offshoot of our target life's goals, God, as a Master Weaver, still weaves us into becoming more excellent virtue, and we know it that there is a clear distinction between who we once were, from who we are now.

Christ is the Virtue I speak of here. He is the ornament of holy beauty, the glory of heaven, and the pride of our holy calling. A dream to have the whole of Him is perfect dream. If not, then it is shattered dream.

As much as God is the Master weaver, He is also the Potter, while we are the clay. But, according to Oswald J. Smith, “if the potter cannot make the kind of vessel he wants to make, the reason is that, there is something in the clay that resists His touch. Just as soon as that hindrance has been removed and the clay yields itself absolutely to Him, the potter can make any vessel He desires to make”. Therefore, your level of all-round greatness after reading this book will be dependent on your yieldedness to the potter, and Master Weaver. Will your life be yielded enough to make out of it honourable vessel, by the divine Potter?

Before an encounter with Virtue's oil, your life may have been in the dusk. But, certainly, not after an encounter. Because after an encounter your life sets out as a break of dawn that shines on unto a perfect day. And when you are fully anointed to be the best God has created you to be, you become the virtue for the blessings of others.

Yes, Christ is the Master weaver! He is the source of all-transforming holy power. Just as the sun God has made continually dissipates heat and light to give light to the earth, so Christ's virtue dissipates to give solution to problems. The reason for which often times He would say, ": ...for I perceive, that virtue is gone out of me". (Luke 8:46)

But, beyond just transforming you with this inexhaustible power, He also wills to help you possess it. Dear reader, here is the picture; it is like, instead of someone giving you a cup of water from a well, he helps you gain free access to the well, from where you continually draw water.

If many a dream today has been shattered, then it is either because of late encounter with the Source of virtue or, lack of encounter. Because when the Holy Ghost meets dilapidated character, the result is always grace. Grace in turn, will produce "Charassein." Charassein derives from the root, "To write with a stylus in wet clay (as in cuneiform script) or to engrave on a stone surface", and means, "marked distinctive quality". This spirit-made charassein is what you need in your life to succeed!

I wouldn't want to doubt that you may have already read, or even known what virtue is all about. But the Holy Ghost wants to take you deeper. To some persons, virtue means gifts, to others, it means talents, while some others hold that it is moral excellence.

Before a person gets converted to Christ, it is possible he may have possessed some gifts or talents.

But gifts and talents are not virtue! They could mean possessing the skill or ability to do certain things perfectly. One may have gifts and talents, but still lack Virtue!

Did you know that there are so many gifted and talented people today who are still struggling in life? Therefore, the virtue of God in a man, is more than just gifts and talents. It is a divine lifestyle, motivated by the presence of an inner holy God living out his full nature within him. This kind of virtue is far beyond our own cultural or moral way of doing things. It is God's way of doing things. It is supernatural! It is divine! Gifts and talents cannot beget this divine whatness, but from it, certainly, gifts and talents arise.

Benjamin Carson today tells of his story, "The Gifted Hands", but the real breakthrough started when Christ transformed his spiritual life. He battled with uncontrollable temper, which threatened to ruin his dream. This led him to passionate heartfelt prayers. Miraculously, God heard him, and gave him real transforming virtue. Thereafter, he never recorded any moments he was ever controlled by his temper. He became a master over his temper, through the grace of God! This and lots more God did for him. Today, Ben Carson is a role model Christian of virtue. I believe the ordinary human culture could not have done this! This breakthrough later paved way for him to become a renowned neurosurgeon!

What God does for you when you are saved, is forgive you your sins and accept you as His child. When you then seek his face, in the spirit of meekness, for sanctification and Holy Ghost baptism, He endows you with transforming holy virtue. First, He uproots the old tree bearing wicked fruit, then sows good seed. And as your life like a seed, is being continuously watered by the word of God, you grow up like a well-nourished young plant, to become a good tree, now bearing the fruit of the Holy Spirit. The fruit of the Holy Spirit, well-guarded in the fear of the Lord, is what you need to succeed in life. It is also the primary requirement to enter heaven at last, other requirements may be termed as secondary requirements.

After receiving the Holy Ghost, He instills discipline to all aspects of your life. He, in addition, guides, directs, and empowers you with His own precious gifts and talents, although for His glory, and not yours. If God discovers any self-glory, self-exaltation or pride in anyone, He withdraws from him immediately. His gifts are not for a show, but for God's service. But your service unto God is not to be restricted to the church. You are also to serve God; in the office where you work as a staff, in the school where you study as a student, in the hospital where you care for patients as a doctor, in the law court where you judge as a lawyer, in your company where you work as a contractor, in your business venture where you do business as a business person, and so on... Wherever you find yourself in life, you are there for Divinity through humanity. On the judgment day, you shall be confronted with questions of what you did with the gifts and talents God gave you.

Do you remember the story of the unprofitable servant, whom his master gave a talent? How that he went and hid his talent in the earth? And was cast into outer darkness, and there was weeping and gnashing of teeth? (Matt. 25:14-30). Likewise, when we misuse the gifts and talents God has given us, we end up in the same thread of life as the unprofitable servant.

You are created to live for God's glory. Rick Warren wrote that "...living for God's glory is the greatest achievement you can accomplishment with your life". And so let all you do in both words and deed be done for the glory of God. According to the holy preacher Wesley L. Duewel, "Always ask yourself, what will bring God the most glory?" if it is not for God's glory, then you have no business with it.

Have you read about the account of the virtuous woman in Proverbs 31? The summary of her life is recorded in verse 30-31, "...a woman that feareth the lord . . . and . . . a woman of fruit . . ." Likewise, a virtuous person should be a person of the fear of the Lord, and the fruit of the Spirit.

The fear of the Lord makes you to always put God's glory first, in all you do. Show me a person who feareth the Lord like Joseph, the dreamer, and I will show you a person who is at good terms with destiny. Show me a person whose life mirrors the fruit of the Spirit like Paul, the apostle, and I will show you a person at good terms with great accomplishments.

Scripture also reveals in the same chapter of Proverbs earlier mentioned, in verse 29, that, "many daughters have done virtuously, but thou excellest them all". What does this scripture mean, invariably? It means that there are many virtues in life, but there is a more excellent one. Today, you can go for the more excellent virtue and be blessed forever. You not only will be blessed, but also you will be a blessing to your generation. Yes, Christ is the virtue of God in a yielded man; to heal, to breakthrough, and to make shattered dream alive again!

GOD CHASERS ARE VIRTUE CHASERS

Many, today, are chasing after world's gold,
at the expense of God.
But all are like chasing the winds. But, oh
Christian chase! Chase now like King David,
chase after the uncommon virtue;

And like King Daniel, chase after the incorruptible virtue!

The glories of earthly beauty fadeth away, when comes the eventides. Such chase not! Chase after
the virtue of heaven, the glories of which only humble hearts can find.

Oh, but wait! How important it is that you know;
there is limit to where your race can take you,
but where grace can take you, there is no limit.
Ask in faith, and receive, for you can be filled
with ever-increasing grace,
to sustain His virtue!

CHAPTER TWO

THE BIG QUESTION

Receiving a miracle from the Lord may come at any divine encounter. But possessing a true life-transforming virtue, from where great miracles are wrought, does not come on the spur of the moment. It will take a whole long time of having known how to sit at the feet of Jesus to learn, to be like Him, and be able to do the things which He did. It will take an in-depth knowledge about the Holy Ghost to understand the dimensions of the power required to help you. You are to grow in your knowledge of the Holy Ghost, as much as you grow in your knowledge of the Lord. Hear Benny Hinn out, at the time he was getting to know about the Holy Ghost: "my search of the scripture went on day after day for weeks – until all my questions were answered. All the time I was getting to know the Holy Spirit better. And that communication has never stopped to this day. I realized He was right here with me".

How can you do like the Lord whom you do not know? How can you possess the virtue of the one whom you do not desire intimate relationship with? How can He even help you reach your dreams, when you both are not close? He wants to give your life a meaning, but each time He tries, distance becomes a barrier.

Today, millions of people around the world are placing their desires and value upon things that are, either of little or, of no eternal worth. No one really takes the time to seek after God. So, how do they find Him? None desires intimate walk with Him, so, how do they know Him? It is like a pilot who has a particular destination in mind, but never has the right compass to navigate his way through. So, how then will he get to his target destination?

The big question is this, "Are you in such a close relationship with God, that makes helping you become easy?" "Do you have such passion for God, than you have for anything else?" How about passion for the Holy Ghost? Is He your number one passion? No level of passion for your life's pursuit yet, should be able to steal your passion for God, and His Spirit.

For scholars, some may require college grades to breakthrough in life, while others may not. But you must remember this, that your success in life is not really a measure of your grades while in college, but the measure of your grace. Yes, men of grace are never moved by their grades! Where men of grades may not stand, men of grace will. All you may need to succeed in life, may just be grace, and not necessarily grades! The grace of God in your speech, the grace of God in your mannerism, the grace of God in your character, and the grace of God in your demeanor.

Hear me; God delights to make something meaningful out of your life. More than your dreams, He, as a master weaver, wants to correct all the errors of your life, and weave you into becoming something more splendous.

See, life is too temporary to waste it on Christless things! Heaven is too busy to invest on; loveless minds, faithless seekers, peaceless rivals, calmless strives, impatient deciders, unlending lovers, and intemperate tempers!

It is time to come into intimate relationship with Christ, if you are still far away from Him; to receive the Holy Ghost, if you have not yet received Him; and to win souls for God, for he that winneth soul is wise. (Proverbs 11:30).

As a Christian, it is important we examine daily how we live our lives. Because people are more inclined to live by the way we live, than by the way we preach. Leonard Ravenhill wrote, "One doesn't need to be spiritual to preach, to deliver sermon of homiletical perfection and exegetical exactitude". But one sure needs to be spiritual to live like Christ. We cannot have sticks of cigarettes in our mouths or, bottles of alcohol all around us, while claiming to stand for virtue. We cannot have fleets of women around us, on the unholy altar of adultery, while claiming to stand for virtue. Get a picture of who our Christ is. He is real. And they that will follow Him, will have to do so, both in truth and in spirit!

LET'S SAY THIS PRAYER TOGETHER

Lord of all grace, I come now in humble surrender,

to seek your face; for so you said, that there are
many virtues in life; but all leads to destruction.
Thou alone art the true virtue,
which leads to eternal life.

Now, save me from the shame of sin,
through thy name; Sanctify me from the
traits of impurity, through thy spirit;

Teach me to distinguish myself from the world,
through thy word;
To bear thy face, through thy grace.
Thank you Lord, for never will I be the same again,
in your name I pray. Amen.

CHAPTER THREE

LOVE WILL WAKEN THE DEAD

"...behold, how He loved him," the Jews said (Jn. 11:36). But can love meet this need? He had lain in the grave for four days already. The starking reality revealing hopeless situation. But Christ gives His word, "...thy brother shall rise again... I'm the resurrection and the life:..." (Jh 11:24-25). Martha affirms the hopelessness of the situation, "...by this time he stinketh: for he had been dead four days" (vs. 39). Jesus reaffirms His stand, "...said not I unto thee, that, if thou wouldest believe, thou shouldest see the glory of God? (vs. 40).

Jesus already, before that event had established a very close love relationship with the father, that makes hearing His prayers very easy. It was no time to make long prayers. And so, He lifted up His eyes, and said, "Father I thank thee that thou has heard me. And I know that thou hearest me always..." (vs 41-42).

"...And when He had thus spoken, He cried out with a loud voice, Lazarus come forth" (vs. 43). What does His crying out with a loud voice portray? His crying out with a loud voice portrayed His passion for God, His hunger to see God glorified, and His love for Lazarus. And he that was dead came forth, bound hands and feet with grave clothes; and his face was bound about with a napkin. And Jesus said unto them, loose him, and let him go (vs. 44).

Love is a Spirit that wakens the dead. It is a spirit that makes hope alive again.

The flow of Christ's love is like a fresh running stream that never runs dry. It pours down like pure rain. It refreshes like the dew. And inspires like the lilies.

Love is priceless. You cannot bargain it. Christ is the pure stream of love that never runs dry. He is the lily of the valley whose love inspires. Other loves are lesser loves and cannot stand the test of time. But Christ's love endureth forever. Your circumstances can never change His love for you.

True love rests upon 16 marked distinctive qualities, which overtime have been called the 16 pillar of love, by me. While we need faith to overcome the world, we need love to overcome all things. Love therefore, can be likened to a pillar which is in the temple of God (Rev. 3:12), because it overcomes all things!

Michael and His angels overcame the devil, by the blood of the lamb, and by the words of their testimony. The Christian saint also, will have to overcome the devil, by the blood of the lamb, and by the words of his testimony. The blood of the lamb is the product of God's love (Jh 3:16).

These 16 pillar of love include: love – suffereth long, is kind, envieth not, vaunteth not itself, not puffed up, not behave itself unseemly, seeketh not her own, not easily provoked, thinketh no evil, rejoiceth not in iniquity, rejoiceth in the truth, bearest all things, believeth all things, endureth all things, hopeth all things, and never fails (1 Corinth. 13:4-8).

These sixteen virtues is expressed within a person, as whole. And so you cannot have one, and not the other. It is just like someone walking up to you to say, "I' am puffed up, but not easily provoked or, I envieth not, but does not suffer long." Of course, you know this is contradictory! It is unscriptural! If you are not puffed up, then you shouldn't be easily provoked too. And if you envy not, then you should suffer long also. Why? Because these virtue come from one spirit as whole, and not as part - from the spirit of Lord! The spirit of God does not express one, and not be able to express the others too.

Love paralysis strife. It cripples pride, because it is not puffed up. It incapacitates hate. And heals deep wounds. It mends broken hearts. Love is the balm in Gilead!

The spirit of love inspired the holy writs of the scripture, and in love we fulfill the law and prophets (Matt. 22:40).

Now, can there be such thing as love in giving? Yes, there is love in giving. But love is far more than giving. Because it is possible to give without love, but it is not possible to love without giving. God did not first give His son before loving the world. Rather, He first loved the world before giving His son. Love should come first before giving. Your giving should be motivated by love. In fact, the rule is "don't give if you don't have love." But I don't think any genuine believer would not give for the lack of love. All genuine Christians have the love that gives!

How about gifts and love? I've talked about gifts in the introductory chapter. But may I still add that; gifts without love profiteth nothing (1 Cor. 13:1-3). We cannot lay claims of the gifts of God, if we do not manifest genuine love. "Covert earnestly all gifts, but I show you the more excellent way, love" (1 Cor. 12:31).

True love cannot be hidden. It will always reflect in your words, and in your choice of words, what we call diction. Also, it will always reflect in your character, and thought life, too.

When Christ was on earth, His life was so full of love that it became apparent to the Jews (Jh 11:36).

Love is light, and whenever it shines, people around see it.

Dear reader, how many people have you being a blessing to by your love? And how much? Is there anyone in your life you don't love? See, if there is one person on earth, of the world's population, that you do not love, then your love means nothing to God.

How great does your love prove to be? The Jews comment about Christ love for Lazarus was "see how much He loved him" (Jn 11:36). What are people's comments about your love life? How much of Christ love can you give to a loveless world, where hate and strife abound?

How about love for enemies? Do you love your enemies or, you hate them? Have you received grace enough to love even your enemies? (Matt. 5:44).

How about love for the brethren? What do you sacrifice each day because of your love for the brethren? Because love makes sacrifices.

How about love for sinners? How far can you go in saving a soul? When a person is resistant to your message about Christ, do you easily give up?

How about addicts? Do you pray for habitual smokers, alcohol addicts, hawkers, bandits, and women given to prostitution, that the chain of addiction be broken?

Dear Christian reader, you need love to succeed. Love is required in all areas of life. Doctors need love, to treat and care for their patients. Lawyers need love, to defend the guiltless. Preachers need love, to preach the truth always, without adulterating it. And whatever dream God has given you, you equally need love to succeed!

My dream is alive

For the sake of love He was born,
and bore the wounds that healed me;
For the sake of love, He was forsaken
on the cross, so the Father might not forsake me;

His love is fiery, a holy fire, a wonder,
and a power that saves me;
Now, death has no claims, nor grip on me,
for Jesus has died, and has risen again.
And my dream is alive, because Jesus gave me. Amen!

CHAPTER FOUR

FAITH CONQUERS EVEN THROUGH THE WATERS DEEP

A Chemistry Professor got into the laboratory with some of his students for an experiment. He had already told his students what would be the result of a titration experiment, based on the expected colour changes. The students believed the professor, followed the right procedures, and arrived at the correct result. The students' faith had produced result! But the students had acted upon their believe to have produced results, for faith without work is dead (James 2:17).

Let's approach this now from the spiritual perspective. God the maker of Professors and scientists, has given His Word. And His Word has proven ever true. If human experiments prove true, in spite of his imperfections, then how much more God's? All you need to do as His child is believe His Word, and beyond every reasonable doubt, you will have the result. Although God does not need to go through the tedious processes of carrying out experiments, establishing hypotheses, or arriving at laws, just to work. In His omniscient power, all He needs to do is speak the Word, and all you need to do is believe the Word, and you will have the result. Kenneth Hagin wrote that, "it is the word of God that produces results!" What result are you expecting from life? It is your faith that would determine the outcome. According to Charles Finney, "…no works are good works, or are in any sense acceptable to God, unless they proceed from faith…" For without faith it is impossible to please God (Heb. 11:6).

"…look now towards heaven and tell the stars, if thou be able to number them: And he said unto him, so shall thy seed be. And he believed in the Lord and He counted it to him for righteousness" (Gen. 15:5-6). This was Abram expressing his faith in a great and perfect God who cannot lie. He was a student in God's school of faith. Today, he has been promoted by God to be the father of many nations, through faith. Yes, God honours faith!

Faith is an unwavering believe in the spoken Word of God, until invisible breakthroughs start becoming visible.

You require faith to hear from God, like Abram did. But you require even a greater dimension of faith to believe Him, in the face of situations that seem to spell impossibilities.

We all have big dreams, big goals, and big aspirations. Some, like James and his brother John, even desire greatness in the kingdom of heaven. All these are beautiful! But at times the road to actualizing them seems rough. And only faith in God could drive one safely, and take one there.

That faith honours God which believes the word of the Lord, regardless of the prevailing circumstances. When Abram believed God and it was counted unto him for righteousness, it was the faith that looked down on the circumstances, and dared to take God at His word.

Dear esteemed reader, in the road to success, you dare not lack faith. Faith is an all-essential key to success. And it displeases God when through faithlessness we fail to reach the height He has planned for us (Heb. 11:6).

Real faith conquers, even through the waters deep. Faith never despairs in life. It never gives up. And never remains stagnant, but keeps moving. Faith has eyes to still see hope in cases of seemingly dead and hopeless situation.

When they came to Jesus that the daughter of a certain ruler of the synagogue was dead, Jesus said unto they that were in the house, "why make ye this ado and weep? The damsel is not dead but sleepest" (Mark 5: 35; 38).

Damsel in that context stands for divine:

D = Dream

A	=	Ability
M	=	Ministry
S	=	Star
E	=	Ensign
L	=	Light.

While others were seeing a dead damsel, Christ was seeing divine; Dream, Ability, Ministry, Star, Ensign, and Light, that was to live again! Then in verse 41 of the same chapter, He took the damsel by the hand, and said unto her, *Talitha cumi*, which is being interpreted, *damsel*, I say unto thee *arise*. And immediately the damsel arose and walked, and the people were astonished. Living faith, therefore, never despairs, even in the face of seemingly dead and hopeless situation.

According to E. M. Bounds, "Faith moves God and God moves mountain". Wesley Duewel wrote that, "Praying without faith is no better than a mere chit-chat". It is the prayer mixed with faith which honours God, and God, in turn, honours His words, by sending prayer answers.

There is a kind of faith that saves us from sin, called salvation faith. This is faith that believes Christ with the heart, and confesses Him with the mouth, unto salvation.

There is yet another kind of faith used for battle, called offensive and defensive faith. This is faith one wields as shield. These two great spiritual dimensions of faith are a necessity to actualizing any dream God has given you. First, you must have been saved by grace, secondly, you must always wield faith as shield, as the world is a battle field.

Our daily walk with God is to be that of faith. Faith does not necessarily need to see before believing. Because our Christ is a faithful shephered.

By gazing unto Him through the eyes of faith for providence, you should never lack, because He makes you lie down in green pastures. Through salvation faith, you should never perish, because He restores your soul, and leads you in the path of righteousness for His name sake.

Through faith for safety; your life should be safe, because when you walk through the valley of the shadow of death God is with you, the reason for which you should fear no evil.

Through chastening faith, you should know neither shame nor sorrow, because the Lord's rod and staff comforts you. Through faith for all-sufficiency, you should never beg bread, because He prepares a table before you in the presence of your enemies.

Through faith for anointing, your head should never lack oil, because He anoints your head with oil. Through faith for blessings, your cup should never run dry, because he fills your cup to overflow.

Through faith for your living, you should never lack the favour and good things of life, because God's goodness and mercy follows you all the days of your life, and you should dwell in the house of the Lord forever – all by faith! No wonder scripture says, "the just shall live by faith!" (Gal. 3:11-12).

Faith is a key that opens destiny's door. While prayer gives you access to heaven, faith is the key that actually opens heaven's door (Matt 21:22).

We receive from the Lord, only up to the measure of faith we have in Him (Matt. 9:29). Nothing so brings down the power of God, as great faith! Likewise, nothing so hinders the move of God's miraculous powers, as the lack of faith (Matt. 17:14-17).

Genuine faith understands the promises of God, and holds on to it, till they are fulfilled. When Christ was on earth, He understood all that were written concerning Him in scriptures. He held on to the promises of God, and God did not fail Him. None even, could alter what was written concerning Him. Likewise, you, too, by faith should believe that none can alter what God has written concerning you (Jh 19:21-22).

God does not invest on a faithless life, or He may be running at a loss. He does kingdom business with men and women of faith. He does not build on a faithless life, or the building will collapse.

When Jesus said unto Peter, "upon this rock I will build my church, and the gates of hell shall not prevail against it" (Matt. 16:18), He was talking about the mountain-moving faith that Peter possessed. Visionary leaders today are men of faith. They are men who have doubts under their feet, to see through the eyes of Christ; men whose dreams ever live unto God; men who will make a move, only if God is willing to go with them!

Voice of Faith

I take no thoughts of what to eat, or drink,
or wherewithal I shall be clothed;
for I know my Source on the throne sits,
and thinks towards me for good!

I know the ravens do not sow, nor reap,
nor gather into barns, yet, He feeds them.
I know He shall much more feed me; therefore,
in Him my faith will live!

I know the lilies of the field do
not toil, nor spin, yet, He makes them grow.
I know He shall much more make me grow;

therefore, in Him my faith will increase!

I know He cloths the grass of the fields,
which today is, and tomorrow is cast into oven.
I know He shall, much more cloth me;
therefore, in Him my faith will stay!

Even Solomon, he said, in all his glory,
was not arrayed like one of these.
I know He shall much more dress
me in glorious apparel; therefore,
in him my faith will live, increase and stay!

CHAPTER FIVE

SELF CONTROL MAKES PALACE THROUGH PRISON

....His dreams were seen as empty, but were later believed. He was thrown into prison, but later rose from prison to palace. A boy who once played about in his coat of many colours, now in a royal garment, with the robe of a king around his waist. A true story! But what was his secret?

He stood face to face with situation that was to decide his fate. He must either choose to defile himself with Potiphar's wife and reap favour temporarily or, choose self-control and face the consequences for a better future. But he held unto the fear of the Lord, the fruit of the Holy Spirit, and a person of virtue. His name is Joseph, the dreamer!

Dear esteemed reader, do you desire to be like Joseph? And to reach your dreams like him? Then, self-control, in matters both small and great, is the answer. Some scholarly authorities have oftentimes used the term discipline for this word. It is one's ability to control one's desires and impulses, or will power, especially when they are tilting towards doing the wrong things.

Notwithstanding, the Spirit of self-control restrains you from making costly mistakes. It keeps you away from danger. *And preserves your life!*

Having the spirit of self-control is like sowing a seed for a better tomorrow. Because dreams are shattered through the lack of it. But are made when like a royal ornaments, we adorn ourselves with it.

Have you self-control? There is self-control in the words we speak. Like apples of gold in pictures of silver, so is a word fitly spoken (Proverbs 25:11). There is also self-control in the kind of wears we put on, the kind places we visit, the kind of friends we keep, the kind of action we display, and in the kind of way we react.

Self-control is important in ministry, in academics, in business – in all areas of life!

Self-control, especially at the time when needed to bring God glory, may be thorn in the flesh, but this will only become a chariot that would carry you to heights of triumph which you could have reached in no other way. According to Hannah Withall Smith, "Joseph had a revelation of his future triumphs and reigning, but the chariots that carried him there looked to the eye of sense like the bitterest failures and defeats. It was a strange road to a kingdom through slavery and prison, and yet by no other road could Joseph have reached his triumph". There are heights you may not be able to attain except through your trials, and your ability to, in self-control, lead godly life in such moments.

Just as after the rain comes the rainbow spreading its beauty to decorate the sky, so also after a self-controlled life, comes a colourful future.

Would you live your today so that your tomorrow can be colourful? And if ever your story is told, let it not be said about you, "oh, see, how he ended, because of lack of self-control, like Samson; but, see, how he ended, like a Prime Minister, because of self-control, like Joseph**".**

Prayer

Dear Lord, be the eyes through which I see,
to navigate through life's rough way;
the ears through which I'm attentive,
to listen out for your voice, meant to guide me.

Be that mind in me, within which your spirit dwells,
to work out your full plan for my life.
Like a professional surgeon, Lord, operate upon my heart;

Remove the heart of carnality, and give a
heart controlled of your spirit,

until thy self-control is established within me,
Lord, give thyself no rest! Amen.

CHAPTER SIX

ENDURANCE WILL REACH THE FINISH LINE

How does endurance as a virtue affects your destiny? Before I give a reply, I think the marathon runners in athletics have a good understanding of this virtue, whenever they engage in the endurance race. Because it is a necessity to reach the finish line, and win the race.

As unsublime as this virtue is, the kingdom of heaven can be attained in no other way, except through it (Matthew 24:13). Also, the road to actualizing some of life's dreams, at times, may be rough, but endurance, surely is the key to getting there!

However, no measure of endurance of man, can match that which the compassionate Holy Spirit bears within us. Because He is the love that endureth all things! Man's endurance is limited to a short while, but the spirit's endurance is unlimited! And as the greatest lover, He also has the greatest endurance.

He feels pains like we do. And can also be inflicted with injury. His heart can be pricked, and he can be grieved. (Ephesians 4:30)

But as a Christian, you do not need to endure all by yourself. It is His holy endurance within you that makes it all blessed. How? By bearing all things for you. And why? Because He knows you are weak, frail and feeble.

The scene behind the passion of Christ perfectly captures the spirit's love and endurance will. Carnal endurance may bring disgrace, but the spirit's endurance will always bring great grace, crowns, honour, and glory. "But we see Jesus who was made a little lower than the angels for the suffering of death, crowned with glory and honour… to make the captain of their salvation perfect through suffering." (Heb. 2:9-10).

The Christian God endures, unlike the gods of the heathen. This is why endurance is God-like virtue. It is not ours to bear. We cannot endure to the point of victory, if the Holy Ghost does not come in. we will fizzle out!

Endurance is not suffering, but a holy life of grace. It is not destructive either. No virtue born of the Holy Ghost is meant to destroy, degrade, or enslave us, matter-of-factly. Rather, it is meant to bring elevation through great grace, crowns, honour and glory. At least if not at the present moment, then in the nearest future.

CHRIST IN ME THE HOPE OF GLORY

For each spiritual battle won on earth,
a crown is reserved in heaven for me;
Grace to endure as a good soldier
Of Jesus Christ, is a means to gain crowns!

Life's battles may throw disgrace
at me; I know the Holy Ghost
My perfect shield, will bring grace;
And when comes dishonor, then will I stand still,

And look up, for I will see Honour
Himself with His innumerable
company of angels on the way, Coming to help me.
And by the grace of God,

I can say, "Christ in me, the
crowns I seek, Christ in me,
The glory I receive, Christ
In me, the honour I believe;
And Christ in me, is the hope of glory!

CHAPTER SEVEN

JOY PREVAILS THROUGH THE PAIN

Sometimes, we find ourselves in some uncharted places where life can become so boring, the starking reality reflecting nothing to be really happy about. We seem to meet unpleasant situations that our joy seems almost gone, and our hope almost lost. And because it seems our dreams is far from being realized, fear and worries soon set in, and we become disorganized and disoriented.

I know that when things are just fine, and the road smooth, one can naturally be joyful. But God wants to meet you, not only at the times when your life is unperturbed and you are joyful, but also at the times when it seems you are troubled and under pressure. He delights to give your life joy and peace.

His joy refreshes you. It livens your dreams. It lifts your spirit. And helps you flourish in the strength of the holy angels (Job 38:7). It is a light of hope that will still shine brightest even in chaos moments. It's an anointing of the Spirit (Isaiah 61:3), and flows out from within you, to others.

According to Scripture, "The Kingdom of God is not meat and drink, but righteous, peace and joy in the

Holy Ghost" (Romans 14:17). God wants to bring you into this kingdom, where dreams are never shattered, but made. Where lives are never lost, but saved. And where already fulfilled dreams, can only get better.

"...the Spirit of the Lord is upon me, because the Lord hath anointed me . . . to give unto them beauty for ashes, the oil of joy for mourning . . . " (Isaiah 11:2). The spirit of the Lord is the oil for our present dispensation. And when He comes upon you, He anoints you with joy, so much joy, to even give to those who mourn (Acts 10:38; Isaiah 61:3).

Paul knew something about this joy. In spite of the bonds and afflictions he suffered while in Jerusalem, he said, "but none of these things move me, neither count I my life dear unto myself, so that I might finish my course with joy..." To Paul joy and ministry were connected. To him if he finished his ministry without joy, then it was no ministry at all.

Joy adds grace to your life and ministry. The grace of God in your life should be palpable, by the oil of joy always flowing out from you.

Joy is heavenly virtue. When the Lord answered Job out of the whirl wind saying "...where was thou when I laid the foundation of the earth...and all the sons of God shouted for joy...?" (Job 38:4-7). What do you think he was doing? He was partly declaring unto Job the atmosphere of heaven – the atmosphere of joy! Today, the experience of heaven has been brought down to earth, in the person of the Holy Ghost.

Then I here men say, "if wishes were horses, then beggars would ride." But I hear the Holy Ghost say "only beggars wish, heirs of God's kingdom do not wish, but possess their possessions. Having the spirit of joy is not a thing to wish. It is a life to live. It is the life of the Holy Spirit. Live it! Because you have it inside you!

Let us pray

Dear Holy Lord, for the sake of your glory,
Christ became a man of sorrow,
acquainted with grief; yet,
He knew no moments His oil of joy
was ever depleted, till His dreams were fulfilled.

Lord, I do not pray for sorrows or grief,
because of my weakness. But if for
your glory, sorrows and
grief do not scare me.

I pray never to know moments when
my oil of joy is ever depleted.
And in the words of thy Holy Son,
I pray now, "not my will Lord,
Thine will be done!" Amen.

CHAPTER EIGHT

PEACE WILL STILL RAGING STORMS

When God gives you a command to embark on an adventure, whatever results from it, it has always being in His holy nature to take full responsibility. Even if it takes walking on the water. Has God given you a dream, or a vision? If you are sure it is coming from God, then go ahead, for your God will take full responsibility.

He constrained His disciples to get into the ship and go to the other side before unto Bethsaida, while He sent the people away. Jesus had never played with His prayer moments, for from thence He harnessed great power to meet people's need. And when He had sent the people away, He departed into a mountain to pray.

Now, the time had come to meet a need. It was no time to pray but to act, "…and He went up unto them into the ship: and the wind ceased…" (Mark 6:45-51). There are times in your life when God requires you pray. And there are times when He requires you act.

He is a specialist in walking upon the sea, if that will be all it takes to save your life. The Holy Ghost descended upon Him like a dove, as a seal of peace upon

His ministry, that even the storms would obey Him. And God so anointed Him, that the winds had no choice, but indeed to obey Him. Because He was, and is, the Son of God, in whom God was, and is, well pleased.

During some turbulent moments in my life, I sought to know about the mystery of this deep inner peace. And as I waited upon the Lord in the place of prayer, He inspired my lips to sing:

Hear these words, coming from
the Lord; Oh ye stubborn storms,
raging thunder storms; Jesus
is the captain; captain of my life;
Jesus is the captain, captain of the ship

Jesus is the captain; captain of His
sheep; storm, storm, storm, oh
stubborn storm; peace be still!
Hear these words, coming from
Our God; oh ye ungodly winds,

raging troubled sea; Jesus is
the captain; captain of my life;
Jesus is the captain; captain of the ship;
Jesus is the captain, captain of
His sheep; storm, storm, storm,
oh stubborn storm; peace be still!

Dear reader, you are never to be afraid, when the Lord of peace is in your ship. For your ship will never sink. You will cross over to the other side safely! For the master has given His word already!

PRAYER

Oh Lord, anoint us with the
oil of peace to preach; so
that fears may be stilled, and
striving cease;

Divine one, endow us with
your bliss to teach with holy zeal,
that we may reap life,
when we sow the good seed.

Good and true all your
virtue prove; yet, for this
one thing we ask now, anoint
us with your own virtue of
peace! Amen!

CHAPTER NINE

GOODNESS SPARKLES THROUGH THE NEED

"… As I watched those beautiful bed of pinks dance, in the soft music played by the cool breeze, that lovely morning, I saw God's goodness in them." Then I thought, if God could be so good to these pretty flowers, then how much more His beloved, the wonderfully created, after His likeness!" You are worth more than a flower! And your life more precious. Jesus affirms that God is God of the living, and not of the dead (Mark 12:27). Although flowers are biologically living, they are spiritually non-living. And so God is even more interested in you, than flowers. He wants to lavish His goodness on you. Because He loves you.

David said, "taste and see that the Lord is good". (Psalm 34:8). It doesn't matter the need of your life. His goodness sparkles through the need!

When someone buys you beautiful cards and flowers, just at the time you needed them, maybe, for decoration or, for encouragement, your countenance is lightened, and your spirit lifted. But God wants to thrill you with more goodness than these. He wants to give you a new song, and fill your heart with songs of praise.

He wills to give you good visions, good ideas, and good thoughts.

Your life is never already too good, to attract the goodness of God. God blessed Abram with a son, Isaac, but that was never good enough, until God had made him the father of all nations!

Faith in God helps you receive a miracle from the Lord. But His unfailing goodness at all times, helps you personalize the miracle that you have received of Him. Because He loves you. And He is good. However, when God does something good in your life, you don't take it for granted. You do not bask about in unthankfulness. He expects appreciation. Don't be like the nine lepers who Jesus cleansed of their leprosy, but never returned to give thanks (Luke 17:11-19). When God gives you clear thoughts, visions, ideas, or dreams, welcome them, then thank Him. Always trust Him to guide you through every single step required to actualize them.

God is good. He still gives good thoughts, good visions, good ideas, good dreams, good gifts, and good life!

CHAPTER TEN

MEEKNESS AND GENTLENESS: THE KEYS THAT CONNECT FACE TO FACE WITH GOD!

I choose to talk about gentleness and meekness in this chapter, because of the relatedness of the terms. Some authorities use them interchangeably. While meekness is called "*praus*" in the Greek, gentleness is called "*prautes*". However, some Greek authorities have oftentimes used "*praus*" for the word "gentle", which shows the relatedness of the two terms.

Jesus is called the Lion of the Tribe of Judah in Revelation 5:5, then in verse, 11, the angels sang ".... Worthy is the Lamb that was slain...." Why was "lamb" chosen by God for illustration, other than the other creatures, like goats or bulls?

God chose a lamb because lambs are submissive. They do not resist the will of the shepherd to ascertain their own will. They have this absolute "not mine will, thy will be done." And can easily and willingly lay down their lives. In other words, they are gentle, and they are meek.

Jesus was qualified by God to be called a divine lamb, that takes away the sins of the world. He was not without dreams and visions when he came down to the earth. And all His dreams and visions not only came true, but Himself became the fulfilling and fulfillment of our dreams, both for the now, and for eternity to come.

You also need this spirit of meekness and gentleness to fulfill your own dreams too. How gentleness and meekness turns lives around! God resists the proud, but gives grace to the humble.

Meekness brings you face to face with God. Moses the man of God knew the Lord face to face, primarily because he was very meek, even above all the men which were upon the face of the earth, B.C.

May I now shock you, dear reader. Do you know that actualizing some of life's dreams may not be possible, until you are able to connect face to face with the Lord in prayers. God reveals Himself only to humble spirits.

Have you come across this scripture that says, "blessed are the meek, for they shall inherit the earth?" (Matt. 5:5). Which earth do you think Christ talks about here? Let's search the scripture: "Ask of me and I shall give thee the heathen for thine inheritance, and the uttermost parts of the earth for thine possession." The earth here can no more but be referred, to those heathen lands and nations where there are false worships of evil deities, as opposed to the worship of the true God.

You may be sent to such strange places, on a special assignment, maybe, as a student, for youth service, or as a missionary, for missionary work. God says to you, "Ask of me, and I shall give thee the heathen for thine inheritance, and the uttermost part of the earth for thine possession. Thou shall break them with a rod of iron, thou shall dash them in pieces like a potter's vessel" (Psalm 2:8-9). This is the earth Christ refers you are to inherit, in the spirit of meekness!

Achieving success in life, at times, may not be possible until you are able to break through such strange places, through prevailing prayers. And the combined virtue of meekness and gentleness, is what connects you face to face with God, before faith comes in. First, you must have a spirit humble enough to stand before God in prayers, before exercising your faith in Him.

However, dear reader, God says unto you, just as He said unto Joshua, "be courageous". Be faithful to Him. And your dreams will come true! (Joshua 1:8).

CHAPTER ELEVEN

THE FEAR OF THE LORD WILL GUARD YOU!

As you dream big, and think big in life, you need practical application of the knowledge you have acquired over the years to actualize these dreams. Your practical application of knowledge is called wisdom. But where does this wisdom come from? Scripture has answers, "…but if you have bitter envying and strife in your hearts, glory not, and lie not against the truth. This wisdom descended not from above, but is earthly, sensual, devilish. But the wisdom that comes from above is first pure, then peaceable, gentle and easy to be entreated, full of mercy and good fruits, without partiality and without hypocrisy" (James 3:14-17). This scripture answers the question of "where does wisdom come from?" Wisdom comes from above!

How then is wisdom gotten? First, through the fear of the Lord. For the fear of the Lord is the beginning of wisdom (Psalm 111:10; Proverbs 9:10). Secondly, by asking the Lord in prayer. For he that lacketh wisdom, let him ask of the Lord who giveth liberally (James 1:5).

One of the seven Spirit of God is the spirit of the fear of the Lord (Isaiah 11:2).

The spirit of the fear of the Lord makes you hate evil, pride, arrogance, evil ways, and froward speech (Proverbs 8:13).

By the fear of the Lord wisdom is gotten. And by wisdom, princes rule, and nobles, even all the judges of the earth. Riches and honour also come from the wisdom of God. But riches and honour are not to be measured by the amount of material things you possess, but by the wealth of your knowledge about God.

God's wisdom is better than rubies; and all the things that may be desired are not to be compared to it (Proverbs 8:11; 16-18).

Solomon asked God for wisdom and God honoured his request. But also added other things to it. Because his prayers pleased the Lord. Those who seek after wisdom are not greedy of the material things of life. Their quest for sage is to mete our sound judgment with holy discretion, and not for material benefits. And that was why God honoured Solomon's prayer. By the fear of the Lord wisdom is gotten, and by wisdom your foundation standeth sure. Honour all men, love your brethren, but fear God (1 Peter 2:17).

Dear reader, it is time to meditate on the things which you have read so far, right from the introductory chapter. Whether you think your life and dreams are already too good or, not, when virtue's oil comes upon you, change is inevitable. That change you already have inside you. If you believed it, then you received it! If you received it, then you can live it! And if you can live it, then you can explore it! Trust in the Lord, and lean not on your abilities. Rest on His Word, and in the power of His Spirit. Allow Him take you higher. For you cannot do it all by your strength. You need the grace of God to prevail. Remember, what matters is not who you want to be, but who God wants to help you become!

TO YOU MY READER

The virtue that had always done the miracle, is one often overlooked by men in the course of history! So unsublime our virtue looks, yet carries such great potentials satan cannot resist.

Christ came simple, unimportant, and nothing to desire about Him. Yet, it pleased God that in Him the virtue for the healing of man's soul dwells.

As I wondered from the book of Revelation which I read, why God chose to include "Topaz" among the 12 stones for building the foundation of heaven, because topaz is simply a silica mineral of aluminum and fluorine usually tinted by impurities, and cannot be comparable to other minerals, such as gold. The Spirit of the Lord replied, "I chose it because it may often be overlooked as unimportant in the sight of men, but not in the sight of God, comparably to other minerals. And because nothing else indeed can play the role of that which seems unimportant, the unimportant, thus, has become important! It is God who makes things important through use! Likewise, it is God who makes men important through their yieldedness for use!"

This is exactly what God wants to make out of your life, my dear reader. Though you may appear unimportant in the sight of men, God sees you as important! No wonder scripture says that, God has chosen the foolish things of the world to confound the wise; and God has chosen the weak things of the world to confound the things which are mighty (1 Corinthians 1:27).

The Spirit of the Lord continues: "There is, therefore, really nothing unimportant about "Topaz" as you may think. Topaz is as important as any other stones of heaven. I believe when you get to heaven, you will understand the difference between the "Topaz of the earth" and the "Topaz of heaven"! The "topaz of heaven" is a beauty indescribable, clear as crystal precious stone, free of all forms of impurities, unlike the "Topaz of the earth" which has impurities in it".

Therefore, when God touches the life of a man, He makes him such a beauty, free of all impurities, that you know it, that indeed there has been a Master's touch!

References

Ben Carson, (1990). *Gifted Hands.* 1st rev. ed. Michigan: Zondervan; p224.

Benny Hinn, (1982). *Good Morning Holy Spirit.* 1st rev. ed. Nashville, Tennessee: Thomas Nelson, Inc; p194.

Bounds E. M., (1997). *Prayer.* 1st rev. ed. New Kensington: Whitaker House; p662.

Charles F., (1999). *Faith.* 1st rev. ed. New Kensington: Whitaker House; p 188.

Hannah W. S., (1888). *The Christian Secret of a Happy Life.* 1st rev. ed. Norwest Nazarene: Christian Witness Co; p 321.

Kenneth W. H., (1993). *Speak to Your Mountain.* USA: Keneth Hogin Ministries, Inc; p217

Leonard Ravenhill, (1959). *Why Revival Tarries.* 1st rev. ed. Minneapolis: Betany House Publisher; p168.

Oswald J. S., (1932). *The Man God Uses.* 1st rev. ed. Basingstoke, Hants, USA: Lakeland; p224.

Rick Warren, (2002). *The Purpose Driven Life.* 1st rev. ed. Michigan Zondervan; p334.

Wesley L. D., (1997). *Measure your Life*. 1st rev. ed. Greenwood, Indiana, USA: Duewel Literature Trust, Inc; p 224.

ABOUT THE AUTHOR

O'Brian Wisdom Chukwumaechi is humbly an Evangelist, and a revivalist. He is schooled at The University of Nsukka, Nigeria and The University of Calabar, Nigeria, and he is currently the founder of Peace Global Revival Networks (PGRN)

www.ingramcontent.com/pod-product-compliance
Lightning Source LLC
LaVergne TN
LVHW090128160826
845673LV00015B/1111

* 9 7 8 9 7 8 7 8 9 0 8 4 4 *